W9-AZS-557

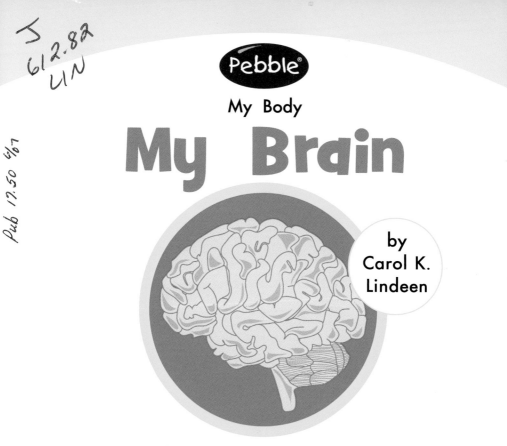

Pebble®

My Body

My Brain

by
Carol K.
Lindeen

Consulting Editor: Gail Saunders-Smith, PhD

Consultant: James R. Hubbard, MD
Fellow in the American Academy of Pediatrics
Iowa Medical Society, West Des Moines, Iowa

Capstone
press

Mankato, Minnesota

Pebble Books are published by Capstone Press,
151 Good Counsel Drive, P.O. Box 669, Mankato, Minnesota 56002.
www.capstonepress.com

1 2 3 4 5 6 12 11 10 09 08 07

Library of Congress Cataloging-in-Publication Data
Lindeen, Carol, 1976–
    My Brain / by Carol K. Lindeen.
    p. cm.—(Pebble Books. My body)
    Summary: "Simple text and photographs describe the brain, what it does,
and how it works"—Provided by publisher.
    Includes bibliographical references and index.
    ISBN-13: 978-0-7368-6693-4 (hardcover)
    ISBN-10: 0-7368-6693-0 (hardcover)
    ISBN-13: 978-0-7368-7837-1 (softcover pbk.)
    ISBN-10: 0-7368-7837-8 (softcover pbk.)
    1. Brain—Juvenile literature. I. Title. II. Series.
QP376.L575 2007
612.8'2—dc22   2006027842

Note to Parents and Teachers

The My Body set supports national science standards related to
anatomy and the basic structure and function of the human body.
This book describes and illustrates the brain. The photographs
support early readers in understanding the text. The repetition
of words and phrases helps early readers learn new words. This
book also introduces early readers to subject-specific vocabulary
words, which are defined in the Glossary section. Early readers
may need assistance to read some words and to use the Table of
Contents, Glossary, Read More, Internet Sites, and Index sections
of the book.

Table of Contents

My Brain. 5

On the Inside. 11

My Brain at Work. 19

Glossary 22

Read More 23

Internet Sites. 23

Index 24

My Brain

My brain is in charge
of my whole body.
It tells me when things
are hot or cold.

My brain
helps me choose
a treat to eat.
I think strawberry
looks best.

My brain remembers
the way to the park.
I wear a helmet
to protect my head.

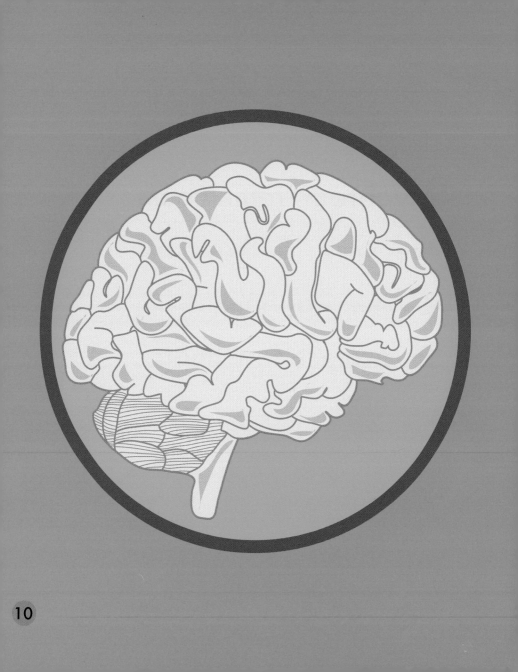

On the Inside

My brain is
soft and wrinkled.
It looks like
a big gray walnut.

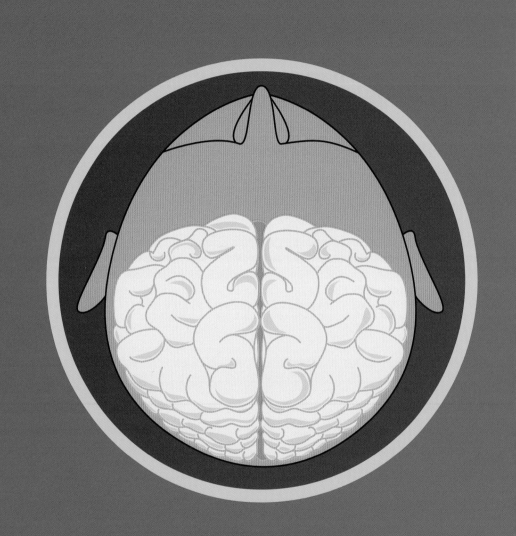

My brain has a left half
and a right half.
My brain grows
along with the rest
of my body.

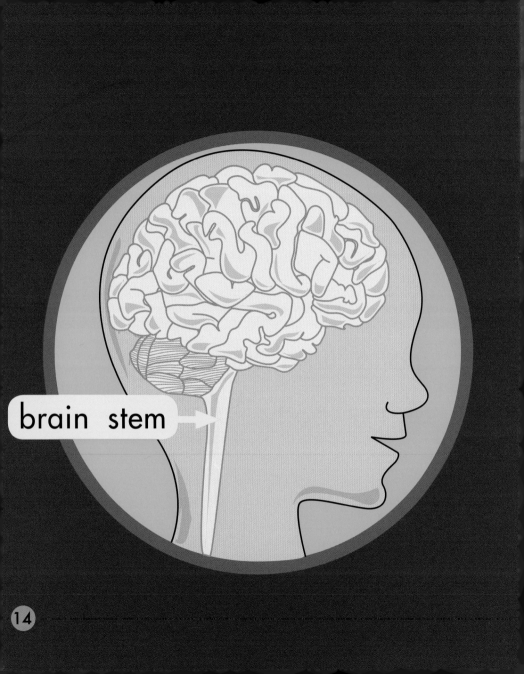

brain stem →

My brain stem
is on the bottom
of my brain.
The brain stem joins
to my spinal cord.

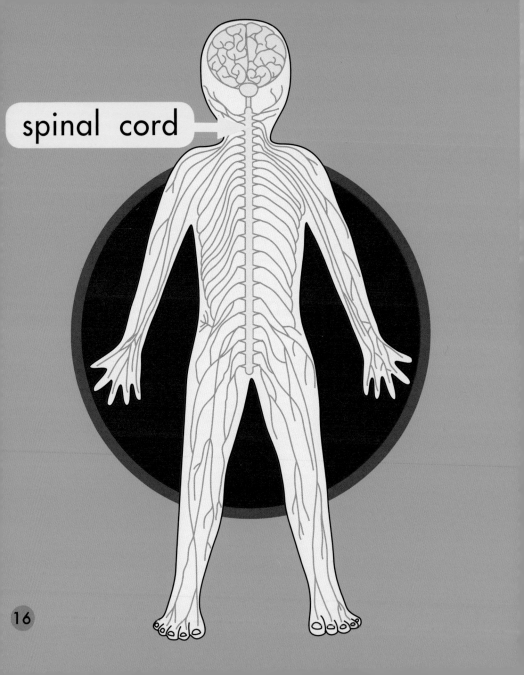

spinal cord

My spinal cord
and nerves
help my brain send
and receive messages.

My Brain at Work

Each part of my brain
helps do different jobs.
The left half
helps me do math.
The right half
helps me draw.

My brain helps keep
my heart beating.
It keeps
my lungs working.
My brain works even
when I sleep.

Glossary

brain stem—the lower part of the brain

heart—the body part in your chest that pumps blood throughout your body

nerves—stringy bands of tissue that connect and carry signals from different body parts to the brain

protect—to keep from harm

spinal cord—a strip of tissue that connects to the brain and runs down along the back, inside the backbone; the spinal cord carries messages between the brain and nerves.

wrinkled—having folds or creases on the surface

Read More

Gray, Susan H. *The Brain.* The Human Body. Chanhassen, Minn.: Child's World, 2006.

Green, Jen. *Brain and Senses.* Your Body and Health. Mankato, Minn.: Stargazer Books, 2006.

Internet Sites

FactHound offers a safe, fun way to find Internet sites related to this book. All of the sites on FactHound have been researched by our staff.

Here's how:

1. Visit *www.facthound.com*
2. Choose your grade level.
3. Type in this book ID **0736866930** for age-appropriate sites. You may also browse subjects by clicking on letters, or by clicking on pictures and words.
4. Click on the **Fetch It** button.

FactHound will fetch the best sites for you!

Index

brain stem, 15
growing, 13
heart, 21
left half, 13, 19
lungs, 21
messages, 17
nerves, 17

protecting, 9
remembering, 9
right half, 13, 19
sleeping, 21
soft, 11
spinal cord, 15, 17
wrinkled, 11

Word Count: 152
Grade: 1
Early-Intervention Level: 14

Editorial Credits
Mari Schuh, editor; Bobbi J. Wyss, designer; Sandy D'Antonio, illustrator;
    Kelly Garvin, photo stylist

Photo Credits
Capstone Press/Karon Dubke, all

24